Ganesh Book

Immortal Ray Productions
301 Tingey Street SE
Washington D.C. 20003
markus@markusray.com
www.markusray.com

ISBN: 978-0-9916277-8-3 (paperback)
ISBN: 978-0-9916277-9-0 (e-book)

Little Ganesh Book

For Removing Big Obstacles

By
Markus Ray

Immortal Ray Productions
Nashville Washington D.C.

A Dedication

I dedicate this book to my teacher Tara Singh. His love of Wisdom touched my heart. These expressions come from this relationship. He was the "remover of obstacles" in me, and thus became my Spiritual Master for life. He was the embodiment of true words that dissolved my false ones. He was a source of light, and continues to impart the light of inspiration that liberates me from illusions. He was the "Star Lion," placed well in the constellations of Spiritual Masters I have known.

Contents

Introduction

A friend gave Markus a tiny Ganesh and he immediately loved it as it is pocket size. Therefore Markus always carries it with him. Knowing that Ganesh is the one who removes obstacles, I have seen Markus take it out of his pocket and set it on the counter, especially at airports. This was funny because I usually had my suitcases overweight so Markus was asking Ganesh to "handle that." I must say it very often worked!

Ganesh is the Lord of success and destroyer of obstacles. This is the most popular deity in India. His large belly is an essential attribute. It is said to contain within all the universes, past, present and future. There are many legends as to why Ganesh has an elephant head. One explained that Ganesh was created by Shiva's laughter. Shiva considered Ganesh to be too alluring so he gave him the head of an elephant and a protruding belly.

Ganesh is often evoked at the beginning of business ventures. He was also known as Brahma's scribe and therefore is the patron of writers. Perfect for Markus! Many people outside of India recognize Ganesh. He is such a character!

There is a real true story that one time when the people were offering milk to a statue of Ganesh, the statue actually drank the milk. This was witnessed by many and it was covered on BBC Television.

—SONDRA RAY

"Today the peace of God envelops me, and I forget all things except His Love."

A Course in Miracles Lesson # 346

This Little Ganesh Book is my homage to the "Remover of Obstacles." Contained within are small one-page entries that remove some part of our thought— any self-deception— whose removal is necessary for us to be free and liberated. So then, we may "forget all things except His Love."

—MARKUS RAY

1.

The obstacles to happiness seem vast, and life is riddled with problems, yet the remover of obstacles is within us to restore our minds to an indestructible peace and joy. The myth of Ganesh becomes real at the instant we banish the *impossible* from our vocabulary.

2.

Forgiveness is the greatest remover of the *impossible* because it erases the memories of doubt formed out of the ruins of failure. Destiny denies obstacles as well, because what is willed to be must be, or it is not a part of destiny. Forgiveness removes, and destiny moves us forward into the mystery of a Life of Action

3.

Action is not of thought because it emanates from the Unknown. Factors of which we are not specifically aware come infinitely into play. This is beyond our thinking and is a Force of Life. Therefore, an Action is the highest movement we can take because it originates from a state of mind that is not subject to obstacles or limitation. Action is a movement of infinite possibilities.

4.

Action is always giving itself to the wholeness of life. Rains fall to nurture all the living things of the earth. Air surrounds the planet with an atmosphere of breathing substance. The person who is of Action does what he does for the benefit of himself and the greater whole as well. He or she gives and receives what is given. One who gives love receives more love. One who forgives can be forgiven also. This is a law of love.

5.

Earth, sea, and sky are blessed with light and the space to be. These are the elemental gifts our Creator has given us to freely enjoy without cost. Love provides these elements that support life and we are always receiving them, no matter what our state of gratitude may be. Gratitude induces a sense of joy, recognizing what is needed is already given. Therefore, gratitude is a major part of the Action of Life, perpetually giving.

6.

The major obstacle to a life of gratitude is fear, and all the memories we hold in our minds that activate and justify fear. Fear and gratitude cannot coexist. Each denies the other. So, we must decide to be in the reality of love, which only knows gratitude; this decision casts out fear. Without fear, the mind can be at peace. Then perception is ruled by a higher observance. It has the power to heal and restore. It can invoke miracles to undo the effects of fear.

7.

Like the gentle force of a sea breeze, the wind of forgiveness blows away the hurtful memories that have accumulated in the atmosphere of our minds. The empty nature of the sky and sea bring solace to the land of thought. Only with thought do we make judgments and fears that cloud over the joy of a clear blue sky. The mind is happy to be emptied, for the breeze to blow away the obscuring overcast. Then the true nature of the mind can be joyous from the light of day.

8.

In Mallorca the light of day is bright and the air is warm. But the sea breeze is always blowing, so the heat is not so oppressive. Little lagoons and bays dot the coastline. Hotels and homes are built on the hillsides above the sea, with balconies and verandas that give people a place to view the remarkable vistas. There is leisure here, and the people are happy. The roads are good and the economy looks prosperous. A visitor is impressed by the pure elements of nature. An island accentuates the relationship of land, sea, and sky—the beauty of life.

9.

The rest from stress and problems, which we seek, is in our minds. Real rest is freedom from problems—a state of divine leisure. Nature is in a rest, even though its movements are vast and powerful. Rest has nothing much to do with sleep. In sleep we go unconscious. But in rest we are acutely aware of the peace surrounding everything. Rest is in the mind, which has no judgments about anything. When the mind is at rest in the present, stillness is observed, even in movements.

10.

To receive the joy and release of the miracles, one needs only to be attentive. Attention is a purer energy than *learning* because it does not have the motive of accumulating knowledge. To be attentive puts one in touch with the present, free of past or future. In the present the given is received. In the present problems are dissolved. In the present miracles and joy permeate all of creation.

11.

The true nature of existence is peace and joy. The duality of thought projects the conflict of opposites, but the peace and joy of the absolute are always present. One's mind has peace and joy in it, yet it also has conflict and sorrow. A decision must be made to transcend the lower regions of thought, to ascend to the emptiness of stillness where the mind is full of God's love. Here the true nature of existence is made apparent. One of peace and joy.

12.

We are alive to the degree we are happy. Life is joyous—totally. In the face of dire circumstances, life presents an opportunity to look past the obstacles toward the ascendance of happiness. Being sad or blue over physical conditions does not erase them. These conditions are showing us the thoughts that need to be released. Forgiveness is the only way to restore us to life. The state of pure joy is the only real state. We must ascend to it.

13.

Judgment, anger, and fear are obstacles to peace. Our judgments are from meaningless thought, which is not real and therefore has no real effects. But we do give meaning to our thoughts, and to see them as *unreal* is a challenge. Tragic events, such as murders, plane crashes, natural disasters, and wars are given immense significance. We judge their *reality*. Not wanting to see them differently, they are kept alive in our minds as memories. To be at peace we need to let thoughts of death go.

14.

Grace is our natural inheritance. Forgiveness wipes away the images that prevent our awareness of Grace. We think we need to struggle and work to survive. The "work ethic" is woven into the fabric of our daily life. Yet Grace is something totally different. *To be* requires no effort, therefore no work. *To be* is to live naturally in a state of Grace. From judgment to Grace requires forgiveness. It is an attention given to correction. Grace corrects all errors by establishing a state of being without them.

15.

We pray to Ganesh to remove the obstacles of the mind. Only thoughts get in the way of happiness. These obstacles can be removed by a willingness to see them for what they are—illusions—and then letting them go. The body and its physical events are only a tool for showing what is real or not real. Pain and sickness are merely the body showing us our minds believe separation is *real*. Health is the Mind of God joining our mind, and influencing the body in truth. In this Action separation has ended.

16.

The certainty of Action comes when there is only one choice to make. An obstacle is a moment of indecision when there are numerous options and the mind is uncertain which to choose. The only one choice to make is to allow the decision to be made by the Higher Self, the Christ. When each instant is given over to Him who *is* clear, the mind is in a state of Grace. He enters where He has been invited to turn the mind around.

17.

A decision to forgive is the only one decision. We don't really know all of the factors and reasons things turn out the way they do. Yet, in the face of problems and disasters great and small, we can say with deeper conviction: God did not create a meaningless world, and so this "disaster" is not real! Giving *substance* to the unsubstantial is very tempting, but the obstacle is our unwillingness to let go of our disappointment and expectations, for "what is."

18.

The obstacles to God Realization are mental. The vision of a realized being looks at the same things with no judgments. At total peace within, having no pressing "needs," he can extend this peaceful vision to others. Problems are dissolved in the presence of a still mind. The way to a still mind takes determination. One must want it more than anything else. External desires have ceased. The one thing needed is acceptance.

19.

Answers are always from the Voice within that has arrived at a place of stillness. This voice does not project solutions; rather, it dissolves the conditions of thought, which made the problem in the first place. Then it leaves the mind empty. When the emptiness pervades one's awareness, there is intense peace in all things observed. This natural state is always there. It is the answer to all problems, in which problems don't exist.

20.

What "comes through" as an expression is determined by the purpose it has. The nature of anything is determined by what it is for. A car is for transporting the body to different locations. A book such as this has a purpose to tell the truth. Words that communicate the truth are helpful. A poet said, "truth is beauty." The ultimate truth that needs to be known is PEACE. To this end are words dedicated—removing thoughts of "non- peace."

21.

A "fasting" of the mind is often necessary to clean up the storehouse of memory. To stop thought, which is not all that easy, requires attention, the likes of which we have seldom known. Usually we give intense attention to a project, to a work task, to a job. But to give attention to silence, which is this "fasting of the mind," is unfamiliar. A teacher is needed then to emphasize the importance of silence and stillness. Without His Light we would not know where the "problem" exists—it is one of the mind.

22.

Peace is always NOW. How fast can you drop your habits of thought? The faster you can drop them, the more you will be at peace now! The sensations of the body are neutral in truth, but we attach such a judgment to almost all of them; therefore, thought is seldom, if ever, neutral. But without this perception of neutrality, peace is not recognizable. The present is distorted into something it is not. The miracle is a cessation of judgments and opinions.

23.

Problems may exhibit very demonstrable effects of pain. What does one do? It is hard to say, "God did not create this pain in my side, and so it is not real," and really get its truth. But, this kind of *denial* is absolutely necessary to be absolved from the subconscious conditions, which made up the "pain" in the first place. The pain may linger, but these "effects" should not be used to postpone the healing of the mind. Forgiveness is total, even amidst the "effects" of symptoms.

24.

People are "stuck" in memory, in past thought. There is no real peace in it. A constant "letting go" is required to be in the present. Anyone can do this, but it is too easy, and thought is addicted to *difficulties*, and problems. So we go on in the quagmire of "thinking," never really having contact with the Peace of the Present. There are no problems in the present. Nothing is left to do. This is a state of mind, which is instantly in heaven. One can decide to be there or not, but the choice is always given. Can we be in the Peace of the Present?

25.

The senses do not need to be denied—but the interpretation of what you sense does need to be relinquished. Then the senses are alert and whole. Beauty is in the acceptance of sensation without the judgments of thought. What one sees, smells, hears, feels and tastes is full of joy and freedom. The body, no longer a limitation, is a means of experiencing the Divine in Matter. This is the true meaning of the Divine Mother.

26.

We are children of spirit, of unlimited Being, having an experience of temporary "limitation." We have been conditioned to think in terms of lack, of a state of "partial" being. Time and space seem to bracket who we are. Yet, these "limitations" can be translated into "another way of seeing." Our movements in time and space are a metaphor for infinite possibilities. In this span of life on earth we have free will to determine these movements, which are always new.

27.

Death brings the movements of the body to an end, as far as we are concerned with the *person*. The body is cremated, sent to a form of dust. These molecules of matter go back into the earth. Once the body has been dispersed through dust, who lives? The spirit imbues the soul with an immortal quality. Is the soul at peace, or is it still connected to conflict? We have a responsibility to be at peace now. "Love which created me is what I am." I know my Self only in a state of inner Peace, which is also Love.

28.

Ganesh removes the obstacles to knowing my Self. My Self is so vast, not dependent on thought or the senses. Experience of the self of personality and memory are often a limitation placed on the Self-Identity of spirit. I am love and infinite being and possibility. Thought gets in the way when it is preoccupied with the past. It distracts me from the present. Ganesh keeps me in the present, aware of my Self. In total safety, I cannot be threatened.

29.

We are afraid of emptiness and stillness. We think we constantly need to be doing something. If not work, then some preoccupation with play—toys. There is a barrage of information. The media is worshipped. No stillness and no end to thinking. With the constant thought process there are inevitable problems. Are we ever free of these problems? “Life has no problems,” say the wise. But we need to be fully attentive and alive to realize this.

30.

The family mind has a grip on the way we live and think. Not only are we affected by how others in the family treated us, we are also affected by how we treated the family. The family mind needs to be transcended or it can be an obstacle to self-realization. Outgrowing the family mind does not mean running away from it, but rather looking at it with the eyes of forgiveness. To step out of the family without judging it is the most challenging act of forgiveness.

31.

Upset, fear, anger, irritation are all memories. Is it possible to have a mind in which these emotions do not come into play? A decision to be free of them is also a decision to be free from memory itself. Attention and determination are required. Who will make this a priority in their life? We are preoccupied with the concerns of making a living, not with outgrowing memory. A still mind is not the goal of most, who would say "why?" But when we see memory is the source of all problems, the solution would be to stop being the victim of it.

32.

We can step out of memory to the extent we see that memory (thought) is the cause of our problems. To be in the present does not require effort. What I sense with the body can be opened to wholeness without a need to cling to any particular experience. When I sit and observe around me there are certain things happening. This observation can be free of interpretation. In this state of no judgment, there is very little memory. What is observed has a natural beauty, even that which previously was judged undesirable.

33.

Why are we irritated at all by anything? If we are irritated by something, then that "something" is more important to us than peace. To have peace, which is to say a mind free of all irritation, it must be valued "above all else." This state of Mind is the reality beyond memory. To value peace above all else requires a vigilance. At the instant an irritation enters the mind, one must say, why do I value this? When I cease to value a certain irritable condition, then peace returns, even when the condition is not met or altered to fit my desires.

34.

There is a peace beyond understanding whose edges are detectable in mental silence. By silence, or the absence of interpretive thought, a person is very aware of the all-pervasive nature of true observation. There are no boundaries or limits. The mind and the body's senses work in unison to free the human being from conflict. This can be called a spiritual awakening. The beauty of this all-pervasive nature comes when thought is still. The presence of peace is apparent. Who would go back to a life with conflict once this peace beyond understanding has been experienced? It is worth one's whole life.

35.

I keep a little brass Ganesh in my pocket. My Inner Child likes it immensely, like an ever-present friend or playmate. In India, the elephant god Ganesh is paid homage. He is the remover of obstacles, and worshipped as such. Whether you believe in Ganesh's powers or not, the aspect of God that removes obstacles is something profound—beyond our thinking. How does the good manifest? What blocks this manifestation? These questions are the formation of Ganesh awareness in our minds. To trust that the good will manifest is the same as worshipping Ganesh, the remover of obstacles.

36.

A teacher is one who points the way out of ego entanglements. We do not know we are "trapped," but the teacher is one who points it out. Either one will be grateful to discover this, or resent the teacher and deny the bondage. Seeing the full extent of the entrapment, the teacher is able to point the doorway out to freedom. But first the student must own the "bondage" and be grateful for seeing it via the teacher. This is the root of reverence. Once this is acknowledged, the student knows that without the love of the teacher, he would have remained in his own prison—perhaps without even knowing it was self-imposed.

37.

To trace one's thoughts and observe their meaning is meditation. *A Course in Miracles* says, "My thoughts do not mean anything." Truly applied, this brings my mind to silence, to empty, to ZERO. The still mind can then observe nature without judgments, thoughts, and memories. What I see, then, in the physical world of form, is innocent, is neutral. This confirms the lesson, "My body is a wholly neutral thing." An observation of my mind in this state has intense beauty. It is not named or divided, but rather connected to the Oneness of Creation. This thought of Oneness transcends the brain.

38.

Gratitude and thanksgiving are the only real prayers. There is no need to ask for things, because trusting God's Grace to provide everything that is necessary removes this entreaty. Stillness has the capacity to receive. I receive the given. This makes me thankful, grateful, at peace with creation. I am happy to extend this gratitude. All those who come into contact with my life are there for me to extend this gratitude. Then life is a song of joy and harmony. Peace has nothing to do with external conditions. It is an inner surrender. It is an inner yearning to give Peace and Joy.

39.

On a plane one can get extremely bored and claustrophobic. Most people read or pre-occupy themselves with some media stimulation. I like to observe my thoughts and sit quietly. Sometimes I jot down my thoughts to see if they make any sense. Often they do. Inner Peace is a state of mind that does not need stimulation or distraction from a feeling of boredom. An acceptance of *what is* lends itself to a quality of inner peace. All aspects of Life are accepted as part of the inner peace. Even another's experience of agitation is enveloped by inner peace. It encompasses everything.

40.

We are united in our gratitude for each other, not by our criticisms and grievances. It is better to appreciate than to attack. There may be qualities and behaviors of another that we do not like, but dwelling on them promotes hard feelings and resentments that only accumulate and fester. People need to be acknowledged for their strengths, not constantly reminded of their weaknesses. Gratitude and praise lift up the soul to higher realms of being, especially when the attributes being praised are true and universal. This is real unity.

41.

We find joy in unity, not in separation. The work of unifying is more noble than the work of tearing down. There is no joy in division. To be "right" by making another "wrong" loses sight of interdependence. Taraji said, "The enemy is not always wrong." He represents the "flip side" of our mind. We hold the polarities of good and bad within us. When these two are owned and unified inside of ourselves, the conflict and division in the world will cease. We will see the *enemy* as our Self, and then there ceases to be an *enemy.*

42.

The mind has a depth and content into which we have not fully tapped. The thoughts we use most of the time are on the thin surface of a vast system of psychic strata. This “crust” is the layer of memory, judgments, opinions—and just the landscape of everyday living. To delve below this solidified mass of thought takes determination to see there is something more. Another way of seeing, without the relied-upon conclusions of what we “know,” liberates us from problems and conflicts. Once one has left behind thought, he is free to access these deeper levels.

43.

At the bottom of the crust of thought are the most hidden densities of experience. Guilt, anger, judgment, fear, negativity, and ingratitude form the conglomerate of the thoughts that attract and record painful and traumatic experiences. Under the crust lies the molten substance of fire that can dissolve the denser crust. This substance is dynamic, ever active, and moving. It is the fire of our existence that keeps us advancing. It will destroy our ignorance. It will remove our obstacles. Jai Ganesh!

44.

People want to be free from the pressures and anxieties of everyday living, but they find themselves entangled in them. Wanting to be free and being free are not the same, obviously. We find ourselves a prisoner of our circumstances, searching for a key to get out of jail within the cell of our own making. What is required to escape from our own *hell*? Many want to be free, but are unwilling to let go of the thoughts and conditions that keep them bound. Any thought which keeps us in *hell* is meaningless. Let it go.

45.

Freedom is instantaneous when you see this: To admit "I don't know how to escape," yet with the conviction that escape is necessary, invokes a higher part of the mind. Then other resources are available—"God is the strength in which I trust." This strength is "in us" but not "of us," therefore, humility and gratefulness are the keys to activating this strength. In this strength lies all freedom, and it is available right now to liberate us. Can we accept it? Do we want freedom above all else, or do we want our problems? We get to choose.

46.

In the space of leisure, there is an opportunity to be free of concerns and doubt. The thoughts of everyday life can be totally put aside. When thought is still, another energy makes itself known. This energy is universal, not personal. It floods into the mind like an ocean into a droplet of water. The boundaries of thought expand to the far reaches of dissolution. In this state of leisure, problems end and the mind encounters Pure Joy.

47.

All things have their Identity in this Joy. A table is inherently happy to serve its function. We take common things for granted, but each has its own life. The wood, the metal, the proportions and design all come together to form a table. Its life in the world may even extend in years far beyond the life of a human, especially if it is beautifully made. It may show wear, but its essence is immortal. Its manifestation may be in time, but its function goes on giving as long as it meets a true need.

48.

A vision is useful to the degree it transforms one's life and brings more joy. The enlightened being is totally free of problems. Problems only exist in the domain of thought, and real vision transcends thought to make contact with a more pure energy of life, which is whole and all-pervasive. Life is not divided, so this vision includes everything in its scope, and forgives all things it hitherto excluded. Vision is of Love, and Life is Love. Nothing, then, is outside real vision.

49.

What would you say to a saint? "My life sucks?" In the presence of a saint, the disparity of the level of inner peace is apparent. The saint is totally still within, and my mind is roaring with problems. So—when am I going to stop projecting problems? These are the concerns of a true aspirant. I ascend only to the degree I see all my problems are totally self-projected. Completion of obligations and agreements is essential. Then one can go to the saint with no agenda, no problems, and no questions. Then he can meet the saint with a still mind.

50.

A little something for the New Year: gratitude for all we have. For the network of relationships around the world; for the high thoughts to which we have been exposed; for the work we do that elevates people spiritually; for our lovely apartment; for our holy relationship; for our future which we place in the hands of God and the Divine Mother; for all of the people who organize events for us; for the breath—the means to connect body and mind with spirit. All these bring intense gratitude.

51.

There is only Pure Joy in reality. Thought falls short of achieving it because Joy is always present, and any movement to "achieve" it is a deviation. Joy is in stillness and silence. These two qualities imbued in any action will automatically produce Joy in the result. Joy is present in the beginning and is sustained throughout the action of life. It is the premise that must be sound—not the "goal." Joy as a precedent eliminates the need for a "goal."

52.

A song to the Divine Mother of Creation to express my Joy to exist: “Oh, Mother, you bless me indeed with eyes that see the multitudes of beautiful things spread infinitely throughout galaxies, on planet earth, my home, that small outpost within the heavens of Your Love. You bless me indeed with a nature such as Yours, a yearning to give form to my ecstasy, the very spark of my life that seeks to give purpose to every action. My purpose is Love, and how could I know its fullness and giving nature without You? “

53.

I move to be ever like You, my Source, that even extends Itself in the dance of light, filling every atom with Identity, all things with their particular forms. In my humanity I join with all, my brothers and sisters alike, all children of the same Mother Divine. All are holy, even the most angry and abject, as they form the entire range of awakening. Oh, Mother, let me not condemn what you created in Love, and so would I receive my own innocence as well.

54.

I paint in the light of Your colors upon the eyes of my devotion. How Your rainbows shine in the sky of half rainy days, reminding me to bear through the drab gray of doubting and uncertainty to catch a glimpse of pure happiness in the arching orange color of Your Love. I set my sights on illumined strokes of painted spectrums as you give my hand the reason to make color my Joy.

55.

Your face is the subject of my ever-striving vision to see things in the light true colors. I can bear the silence of Your Love in the Joy of seeing these rainbows of bright hues in the countenance of things, in Your creative intimations. My hand dips the brush in Your cup or orange; I stroke the canvas with swirls of yellow gold. Your royal purple bestows its poise in the shadows of Your quietude. I am astonished to see You emerge, glistening in a blush of flesh tones before me.

56.

The strokes of Your Love come to me as I follow the movements of the brush that lays down colors of Pure Joy; the ones that compose Your face ever and ever again in the light of liberation. Free are the lines in the countenance that inspires me; I apply paint to the portrait of Your Holiness. The thin glaze of bright orange is the sunlit nectar that washes my intention clean and sparks the glow of molten strands flowing to Your shoulders of glee.

57.

You remove me from my troubles. Without them I receive Your Love upon the pages of my heart; on the pristine parchment the words flow into script to reflect Your presence—in the Holy Book of appreciation that gathers in my chest. It lives and throbs on each leaf of words held to serve only You. My pen is the tiny tool transformed to record a poignant moment of deep listening. How can I love You more in this action of scribing my Joy.

58.

I am ever yours, my love, awaiting the moistened lips of your affections on the heightened crest of my post of passion. The afternoon light floods the space of our togetherness and warms the very nature of our bond. You come upon me on the softened down of pillows that form our couch of conjugal bliss. You delight in the meal of my maleness and I am taken to the explosion of my gratitude, as my gift of pure nectar feeds your happy soul.

59.

I wait for you in silence, listening to my beating heart that anticipates your coming through the open door of my afternoon affections. You are out on a temporary saunter, an errand of daily necessity, as I await your return into my embrace at home, into my deep surrender. The time is too long, my love, that you are apart from my passions that rise to meet you in the region of our holy union. I am ready for you with perfect happiness at the center of my greeting. Hasten home, my love, into your man.

60.

In front of the multitude the inner person becomes apparent. Any insecurities will surface because I could subconsciously be expecting disapproval. But this is only an illusion of myself, not who I really am as God created me. I can present myself in a state of quiet with no judgments at all. This is the approach that has no fear or defense, no insecurity. To awaken the people, I need to be aware myself. This means I am free of self-deceptions and opinions. This state of mind comes from a place unknown. Free of thought, there is Love.

61.

There is nothing to fear, yet the brain is motivated by self-survival. To die to this motivation is to be in a state of no fear. Self-survival protects and defends an image of the self which is "made up." This self is an imposter, yet it appears to have the authority of the "real" self. The conflict this false self contains is tremendous. It is always seeking "something else" to add to the complex of its memory, its experience, its "knowledge." To end this constant search for self-improvement creates space to be silent and still. In this space the God-created Self emerges into awareness. This Self is already perfect, not in need of improvement.

62.

Ganesh is the embodiment of a movement that has divine purpose, and cannot be deterred by distraction. It is fitting that his elephant nature symbolizes a single function that removes any obstacles. He is so strong in the animal kingdom, not even the lion can threaten him nor stop the actions of his nature. Therefore, the elephant becomes part of the attributes of God that give strength and steadiness, that is determined to fulfill its mission, that has faith in Higher Forces which reveal the way. Ganesh is the carrier of destiny, always on track with the Divine.

63.

To surrender to Divine Will is to give up my own agenda. I can "know" the obstacles that prevent me from this surrender, which are disguised as important items in my agenda. When I cease to follow this agenda, I am closer to surrender to the Will of God. In this state of mind, relative "knowledge" has become superfluous. I am removed from the need to "know" anything but God's will—because it acts through me every moment, without a preconceived direction. In this state, the unknown is the great catalyst for Divine Action. From this great Unknown, Absolute Knowledge emerges.

64.

To give a miracle of forgiveness, the mind must be free of judgments. When I think "I know" the truth, I am easily deceived. This is a judgment that blocks forgiveness and the miracle. The real miracle takes us back to an Identity before thought and judgments came about. It is a pristine space of peace and quiet in which Being is untainted by sorrow of any kind. It is a state of Pure Joy that has no opposite and has no need to judge.

65.

All things are Divine. To see the Divine in all things requires an attention that is "mindful of Love," which does not judge. Accepting all things are either expressions of Love, or a call for Love, places Love at the center of real awareness. This awareness is always grateful for whatever it encounters. There is not a moment in which it is not grateful. In this peace and quiet Love covers everything with a blanket of holiness. All are included. In this total inclusion how can there be conflict? Peace and Joy are inevitable results of Love.

66.

The time one spends on this planet is precious time. A destiny to awaken to one's true Identity—Love—is the only real destiny. There are many ways to awaken, but there is only this one goal: to fully realize Self-Identity as Love. Many people never wake up to this one goal because they are entrapped in thoughts of non-Love. The inner impurities need to be cleansed and erased. But this requires attention to do so. The means are provided through forgiveness, but few fully use the means. Forgiveness and Ganesh's removing of obstacles to the awareness of Love's presence are the same.

67.

The separated self is seen as "normal." People have defenses they do not even realize, which result in a closed nature. We walk around contained within personalities and individual space. There is very little opportunity to make real contact with each other for fear it will be seen as obtrusive and inappropriate. So we grow to accept this isolation with the stoic stance that nothing really can be done about it. We are afraid to step outside this social norm. In an ocean of people we feel the most alone. The vibration is one of separation and quiet resignation.

68.

The forgiveness of the Lord is perfect, leaving no tiny tinge of guilt still intact, ever ready to erase the consequences of mistakes made in the deep sleep of separation. Why do we live except to realize the all-encompassing state of Peace and Joy? No particular accomplishments or acquisitions can bestow this. When you come to the end of seeking and learning, there is a place inside that wants nothing. When this internal stillness is reached, no external enticement has any pull. Why would you deviate from an all-pervasive Love of Peace, once you have received Its beatitudes?

69.

There cannot be a problem in a state of the miraculous. This is the nature of the miracle—the suspension of thought's karma or cause and effect—to restore an original state of perfection pre-existing of thought. A problem is a recurring mistake of perception, manifesting as a current condition of experience based on the past. This mistake is a "replaying memory" in the form acted out. The miracle erases the thought causing the problem through forgiveness. This is the only way to be freed from the consequences of memories. The miracle forgets the past.

70.

The body and thought play out certain painful dramas, similar from the past. An "accident" is never without a pre-existing memory reactivated. The body is subject to injury. When one is not careful and attentive, injury can occur. Once there is an injury, restoration is now the principal concern. The Atonement deals with the pre-existing mental condition that "caused" the injury. A thought brought about the "injury", and one needs to erase it through forgiveness. I may feel the pain, but my Self is not engaged in any complaint. It would act to remove the pain. The pain need not be a distraction when forgiveness is present, removing the obstacles of thought. Jai Ganesh!

71.

To disassociate pain from the Self, disorder from order, the mind must be clearly identified with Spirit. That means it is not affected by physical conditions. It observes thought, but only the thoughts of Spirit, of God, of Love, are worthy of identifying with. We can redirect the focus of our thinking. Engaging in conflict is a choice. Forgiveness allows choice to be conflict-free. We choose to be at peace, aligned with Spirit, that our problems cannot be made to dominate the mind. This one choice is essential, even in the experience of pain. It is total unification with Who we are as God created us.

72.

An injury of the body gathers a person's attention (ideally, to focus on the perfection of Life that is always happening, regardless of the injury). Forms come and go. Perfection is always present. Pain is felt, but what effect does that have on reality? Perfection is not dependent on external conditions. All people deserve their basic needs met—food, clothing, shelter, water, cleanliness. All deserve to be pain free. But beyond the basic needs, higher laws give awareness of perfection, in spite of physical injury. In a state of leisure, gratitude and adoration show one's perfection.

73.

To feel the Love of God, a new attention is needed. The gambit of human emotions has a wide range of various feelings. One could feel sad or glad, happy or disappointed. The Love of God is a totally different kind of feeling. It is not subject to fluctuations of moods. The Love of God is a Love for Love itself. Who can have a problem in this state of the Absolute? When Love is really what you feel, how can there be sorrow? We need to wake up to this higher feeling in which all other feelings cease.

74.

A sense of loss is only possible when there is attachment. What is the real state of nonattachment? Spiritual seekers like to talk about nonattachment, but who really is free from the bondage of attachment? We are attached to ideas as well as to images and things. When those things and ideas are taken away, there is a sense of loss and upset. Can there be any upset in a true state of nonattachment? When things are taken away, this is a good test to see how attached we still are. Mostly, we are still attached.

75.

Loss is felt when something important is stolen. The difficulty of replacing an essential item can make a person angry and resentful. But the question should always be one of forgiveness. "What in me attracted this incident of theft?" Either I am "stealing" something from others or I'm feeling "ripped off." In both, I feel a sense of scarcity and not being cared for by the Divine—or protected. Forgiveness is the lesson, but it would have to see my *loss* as a learning tool. Jesus says in *A Course in Miracles,* "Loss is not loss when properly perceived."

76.

When we embrace opposites without a judgment, then the conflict of duality ends. When one stops projecting evil onto others, there is only GOD. Why does the mind engage in conflict, in sorrow, in fear, in the projections of duality? Separation from Oneness makes division real. It is enough to be grateful for the diversity of life and to have reverence for all of it. All is all. The good and the evil stand together. Demons and angels are joined in the vision of the Christ, the forgiven world, a state of heaven.

77.

People have interest in their own gain and call this the pursuit of happiness. Can ambition ever be happy? The weight of accumulated property and wealth is borne on the labors of others, often at the expense of people's life energy. The exploiter and the exploited are bound in a special relationship of self-interest. What happens when I give up all interests? "I do not perceive my own best interests," is Lesson #24 in *A Course in Miracles.* What a relief to be guided away from the greed of self-interest. I can have Peace and Joy without struggle. Isn't that better?

78.

We have not received the gifts of God, obviously, or we would not be so obsessed with loss and gain. The Goliath of financial prominence in our lives rules over the attention we pay to the Spirit, which is our first Identity. Without placing Spirit in the forefront of our endeavors, the separation of mind and body from its Source cannot help but bring about chaos. The gifts of God remain unrealized because the source of true happiness is misplaced. Aligned with Spirit, even financial concerns enhance these gifts; unaligned, they distract from them.

79.

Possession brings about attachment. Attachment misplaces our sense of value onto things—physical and mental. Then there is a possibility of loss which brings about fear. When a loss does occur, we then feel bad. Upset is not a result of loss, but the original sense of possession, which is attachment. This is why the wise encourage us to be nonattached and to simplify our lives to have few possessions. In a life of simplicity there is very little to lose. Then there is a sense of safety. More possession leads to more attachment, and that leads to more fear. Love is free of attachment.

80.

The issue in life is to accept who we are as we were originally created. A finite existence is what most accept. Even billionaires do not escape the limitation of belief in death. No matter what philanthropic foundation left behind, their kingdoms have an edge, a border, a containment. Eventually they die and perhaps their name goes on—the Rockefeller Foundation, the Bill and Melinda Gates Foundation, the Nobel Prize, etc. What we were originally created as does not have an edge, nor does it need a "memorial" to keep it alive. It is Immortality itself.

81.

All that we think we are is not what we are. To strive to know the Self is not the Self. It will never lead to Self-realization. Self-realization is just another “goal” put out there to achieve. The Real Self cannot be achieved, because you already have it. There is nothing to achieve. You can accept or reject this awareness of who you are, but you cannot alter it in any way by this decision of your attention. To be attentive to the benevolent reality of Love and Mercy, you must accept your true being is Love and Mercy. Then enlightenment comes rushing in.

82.

Awareness is merely total attention that has no center. The senses are surrendered to an all-pervasive wholeness. Individual sights, sounds, smells, tastes, and feelings are noticed and released into this wholeness. It is natural to have these sensations, but when the mind does not cling to them, judge them as good or bad, pleasurable or otherwise, a total awareness that has no center, no goal, no prejudice emerges. This total awareness is the home of Love because it includes everything. It does not divide, compare, or distinguish because it accepts and unifies. Jai Ganesh!

83.

Beauty is everywhere. There is no place, no time, in which beauty is not present. Therefore, when I am not aware of beauty, it is because I am not attentive to it. Beauty is free of judgment. It is free of an "aesthetic," a philosophy of beauty. The people who promote and cultivate a sense of beauty are only partially in touch with it. The realization of beauty cannot be cultivated. It comes about when the mind gives up all striving to know and possess beauty. Then it is noticed everywhere. It is always present, always new and unexpected.

84.

The mind in conflict will project an enemy. Once this enemy is "crystallized" in the mind, it is impossible to be at peace and to know the real action of Love. Then life is wasted. Death is the end result of conflict. Do we ever look into our mind enough to root out all conflict? Who is truly at peace? Without peace there is no Love. We make all kinds of substitutes, excuses, and opinions to maintain our position. Who can drop it? We have to make a stand to reject conflict in ourselves. Until we value peace above all else, we will not meet with the Absolute, with Whom we really are.

85.

When the mind lets go of all conflict of any kind, the real purpose of life comes forth. It is an action of deep and abiding Peace. It is not so concerned with "doing," but with "undoing" anything not at peace. Perfection is a state of being that is always present. The vision of this perfection is an inner knowing independent of the senses. Perfection does not need to correct anything. I need only let go of the desire to *fix* myself. "What is" is perfect right now—in whatever form is manifested.

86.

To be in a state of Glory would require deceptions to be finished. Any grievance would block the awareness of Glory. Any tinge of unhappiness would be in opposition to Glory. Glory is always mine, yet I am too preoccupied with lower states of mind that have not risen to It. Forgiveness is the only means by which the lower states can be transcended. To rise above anger, fear, doubt, and upset of every kind, the grace of true forgiveness is needed. In this grace, there is the gift of Glory. Glory is an acknowledgment that I will be the light. Then "mine eyes have seen the Glory of the coming of the Lord."

87.

Truth will correct my mind, yet I need to give my attention to truth for it to erase the errors of memory. I have placed these errors between myself and the Glory I have been given. The dissolution of toxic memories is the function of forgiveness, which is the real reason we are here. Without forgiveness these memories go unchecked, and therefore keep replaying their painful manifestations. "Chronic problems" are just errors I have not really brought to the truth. The "death urge" is much stronger than I think. Therefore some problems are chronic and can go on for a whole lifetime. Truth is much needed.

88.

People want to be free of their past. The sorrow of held memories seems to go on and on. The release of these memories is the function of forgiveness. Without forgiveness, memory stays lodged in the mind repeating itself over and over again. The breath of rebirthing can bring forgiveness to the memory of hurt. The hurt can be neutralized. A state free of sorrow is very possible when the mind is willing to let go of memory and certain habitual thoughts. When there is no judgment, there is neutrality—the ZERO STATE.

89.

In transit, thousands of souls come and go from place to place, from lifetime to lifetime. All over the planet people are born and people pass away in the great cycle of birth and death. Affected and influenced by memory, a soul chooses a family and all the cause and effect relationships that are contained in it. How can there be free will amidst these conditions? There is the function of forgiveness, of mending and healing, which takes on many forms for different people. But the choice is always to forgive or not. In this choice there is free will.

90.

The Gentleness of Creation is observed when I am using the Mind of Gentleness. This Mind of God is my own real mind. There is nothing outside its all-pervasive nature. It contains the seen and unseen, the sensed and that which transcends all senses. In this wholeness there is no conflict between what is and what is not. All come together in Peace. In this state of the Real Mind, Creation is absolutely peaceful and gentle. I am that as well, being an integral part of Creation.

91.

We are in the habit of complaining, finding fault, and holding grievances. This blocks our awareness of peace and joy. Peace and joy are always present, but our minds are preoccupied with conflicts of comparisons. When we compare this versus that, it implies a conflict of desires. I want the good and reject the bad, and I must assess and choose between the two. In this choice there is no real peace. Peace is an effect of one choice: to end all comparison and conflict in the mind. Then I am aware of only what is.

92.

To what voice do we listen—the one of Love or the one of fear? The mind is preoccupied with survival much of the time—earning money, maintaining the body, pursuing desires, etc. Underlying these preoccupations is fear. Reduced down to the most common fear—death—the mind works hard to deny it. It manufactures a career to escape this fear, but eventually illness and old age creep into existence, then death follows anyway. Yet we are Love at our real core. Love looks on death and does not fear, knowing Life is immortal.

93.

There is no Love outside of the full embrace of Life. Life is Love. Life can only bring more Life. The illusion of death is not Love. The entering and exiting of a body does not establish real Identity. Identity precedes birth into a body and goes on after the exit from the body, which we call "death." This extension of Life into non-physical states of being is also an aspect of Love. Yet, Life must be immortal to rise in our awareness to reach Love. We Love when we accept we are only Life. And then there is no *death.*

94.

An amazing environment is above the clouds. Flying over continents one gets a sense of vast expanses of the earth, and this is a sense of freedom, also. We yearn to be free, and being in the sky above the earth is a good metaphor for this freedom. Technology has mastered time and space, reducing how long it takes to travel across immense spaces. In the sky one can ponder this immensity, a small part of the infinite. The universe is large. When I relate to it I see my own vastness as well. Ganesh removes all sense of littleness. Jai Ganesh!

95.

Love is a quality of attention. I can attend to a state of awareness that looks with eyes of total gratitude and acceptance. That which is not at peace can be forgiven, bringing my attention back to Love. Love does not need thought to be Itself. Attention does not project my interpretations onto people, places, and things. I can achieve a sense of Love when I let go of thought completely. I step outside the workings of the brain which is always "thinking," and enter into realms of the Mind, which is totally empty. Yet in this emptiness It contains everything.

96.

Travels on the road produce wonderful relationships. A life of service brings a person to value relationships more than anything else. When the Master said to the fishermen, “Come with me and be fishers of men,” He was lifting them out of a life of survival into a life of Relationships. Survival is mainly concerned with issues of the body. Service is a shift in energy away from personal survival to a collaboration of the Spirit in which we are all joined in common good. This shift is one that puts Relationships in the forefront.

97.

The honoring of the elements—earth, air, fire, water and ether (space)—brings me into harmony with the Divine Mother. Physical creation is the "body" of the Mother, and to honor Her body is to be in harmony with your own physical form. Babaji said, "I leave everything in the hands of the Divine Mother," and then He left His physical body. That is to say all things are manifestations of the Mother. Reverence toward Creation is the same as worship of this cosmic feminine force. OM MATA HARIAKHADI SWARI ! Which is to say, "Hail to the Great Cosmic Mother!"

98.

I AM AS GOD CREATED ME, — as pure Spirit. As one considers the meaning of this statement, it is clear to see most of our thought processes are preoccupied with something we "are not." Spirit is unlimited and forever. It defies description, and it is beyond all form, yet it imbues all form with Life. Life Force and Spirit are the same. Even scientists cannot define Life Force, nor adequately describe its origin. We are certain that Life Force is in us but not of us. When we have this certainty all of Life becomes Pure Joy. Death is overcome. Spirit imbues the body with Life Eternal as well.

99.

What can we truly communicate to another? Can the separation end? What would communication be in the unseparated state? Only the Christ Mind, the Mind of God, is totally clear, free of any separation. What we fail to see is that Christ's Mind is our own real Mind. All other mental preoccupations are dreams. The separation is not real, but "thought" believes it is. So the problem is giving up thought. We are so in the habit of "thinking" we seldom come to the still mind, which is Christ's Mind, which is our Real Mind.

100.

Something original does not copy. So where does *the original* come from? Obviously not from memory. A creative action comes from the Void, a state of mind beyond thought. What is truly new? Freedom from the "known," which is memory, is the only real freedom according to Krishnamurti. There is no way to "get to" the Void. It is always present. Acceptance of the flow of Life, without judgments or preferences, puts one in a state of gratitude. In this state of mind, the Void is very close. It is the source of the Creative.

101.

I am as God created me now, as much as anytime. But my mind is preoccupied with past thoughts, with survival, with the media—things other than my Identity. So I have forgotten who I am while my mind is so active and preoccupied. To be aware of my Identity requires that my mind lets go of concern, fear, anxiety, and motives. It becomes more and more still, empty and quiet. Then I am not limited to thought. I am closer to realizing my Divine Self.

102.

We adorn the body and confuse it for the Self, so much that we can hardly imagine the Self—independent of the body. A mind is made of the conscious and the subconscious, together making up the soul. The content of the soul is my responsibility. When the soul contains only an invocation of the Spirit, letting go of memory that promotes separation, then the soul can meld with the Spirit, with Infinite Intelligence. Then I am free. My soul has joined with the Infinite. This is real Yoga—to join my individual self of my soul with my universal Self of my Spirit. Then I am *in a state for grace forever.*

103.

I am now, or not at all. I am before I manifested a body. I am equally after I manifested a body. The time I am here in this life does not matter to the degree I realize the truth of the I AM. Once I AM certain of my Identity, then extension of this fact to other human beings is my only real function in my life. The I AM presence is everywhere, all of the time, yet a person needs to give it attention in order to be aware of it.

104.

God is the original I AM. I AM has no limits and no manifested form. I AM is no thing, yet it has the energetic potential to manifest anything. I AM manifested as "Markus" or "Sondra" or a mountain or galaxy. It took no less effort for I AM to manifest a galaxy than to manifest a grain of sand. I AM aware of my Identity as a creation of the I AM, having the capacity to co-create through Inspiration from I AM.

105.

The soul without the body is still the soul. What is purified is pure. That which is unchanging is constant, always the same. Purity is something constant and unchanging, so the purified soul is that which does not change. Unaffected by being this way then that way; by living, the pure soul identifies with the essence that is I AM. Immortal, the soul freed from the body is Holy, as it identifies with the All One. In the body it is Holy as well, when the soul connects itself to the Spirit.

106.

The wise sages, or lovers of wisdom, will gradually eliminate the unnecessary from their life. They will simplify themselves and maintain the body as a tool of the Spirit. In the service of the Spirit, they transcend thought and common understanding. They see that knowledge is limited and thought is meaningless. They yearn for the truth and this is revealed in the unknown, the vastness of the unlimited. This Divine Connection could be called *necessary*.

107.

Ganesh removes memory. There is only one thought to remember—I AM LOVE—which is beyond all lesser thoughts. All else needs to be removed as it is impermanent. The purity of the soul that identifies with the spirit can bring the light to those who are "stuck" in the body. I purify my soul by letting go of negative memories and embracing the empty. Love is nothing limited. It is an all-pervading presence of perfect peace enveloping All things.

108.

We spend much of our time waiting for things to come. When *this* happens, then I will be content and fulfilled. So happiness is held off into the future when favorable conditions in my external situation shift my internal mood. This waiting is a fallacy. The present has nothing to do with future conditions nor is it dependent on the past either. What I decide now is all that matters. An upset now is always an error in thinking: I perpetuate a past mistake or fear a future one.

109.

Happiness is only in the present. I may not have ever known it, totally. Yet in the refusal to relive the past or project a future, there is a stillness that can be witnessed. In this stillness of the present, thought is silenced, and the past and future do not dominate the mind. Happiness is the absence of fear and anxiety, cares and worries. What is now is complete and whole, regardless of the residual symptoms and disorders of mis-creation. I AM FORGIVEN, and all I look upon I release as well.

110.

A tinge of discontent for an "external" situation is always a reaction. We try to justify our reactions rather than question the discontent that arises. Why is my mind upset, rejecting peace? At the instant of the upset this reasoning does not occur. What is swifter than thought's reactions? That is the state of mind required to undo them. Peace is superior to reactions of thought. So few have realized this level of the Mind; perhaps Socrates and Jesus, Babaji and Muniraj. We must be determined to go toward it.

111.

Ascension is merely the rising up through the levels of the mind. Levels of age, experience, maturity are part of the ascension process, yet age and experience are no guarantees for ascension. One must question his own mind and the content and quality of it. The inner being needs examination. Impurities of thought that show up as problems need to be neutralized and transmuted through forgiveness. The great "eraser," forgiveness is the means by which I will ascend or not. It is a constant process of "not this, not this, not this."

112.

When I do not want anything other than inner peace and joy, I will have it. This is the real meaning of determination. Thought, intent, reception and acknowledgement are consistent. Another aspect of determination is surrender. Inner peace is an aspect of life, of Self-Identity that is bestowed upon us by our Creator; therefore, it is not something we can "make up." When I am determined to undo all things that are not inner peace, then thought, intent, reception, and acknowledgement are all lined up. Then what is given comes to my awareness, already there.

113.

The wise do not indulge in opinions; their thought is silenced, and they only consider facts. A fact is not from the known, in its purest sense. The essence of Love is not the same as the expression of love. An expression can be misinterpreted by thought, but the essence cannot. The Essence is the real fact, the expression but an effect or mirror of the fact. Cause is the real fact, not the effect. We are taught just the reverse. A fact is Love, which does not react or condemn.

114.

Thought is a prison until one sees it is meaningless. Some thought is necessary for the survival of the body, yet the purposes of life cannot be gleaned by "thinking." The wise begin to silence their thought and give more attention to quietude and stillness. In a world of endless movement the wise reduce their actions down to prayer and service; these, combined, lead to peace.

115.

To realize my Higher Self as God created me, I have to shift my attention to wholeness, a state of mind in which there is no separation. In Spirit there is no separation. The Self which identifies with that which binds all things together is the Higher Self, the Christ Mind. When I forgive the body and the decision making part of my mind, then my soul is aligned with my Spirit, and Grace is restored. The only decision to make is to commend the mind and body over to the Spirit. Then my conscious mind and subconscious mind look toward God for solutions.

116.

Clarity comes in an instant when the mind is disengaged from thought, opinions, desires, etc. An inner peace pervades awareness and it blankets all external observations. In other words, the mind is still, and this stillness affects the senses of everything physical. Inner Peace is the extension. It is what the still mind imparts to the world amid conflict and chaos. All have a responsibility to come to a still mind. That is closest to the Self, the Christ, the being who has realized his Identity is LOVE.

117.

The major obstacle in life is memory. It is the arbitrator of experience until it is neutralized and silenced. Most experience is just a replaying of a memory, though maybe with different players and forms. To be free of memory requires a vigilance of a different sort. This vigilance looks upon the outside and always asks what pre-existing thoughts are manifesting. In this way it is taking responsibility for everything that happens. This is necessary for forgiveness to release me.

118.

Waking up is merely letting go of thought. When the mind is not engaged in assessments of what it observes through the senses, experience is one of peace and joy. It does not matter what the experience is, because all experience is preceded by this still mind that is detached from the externals. Because it is not engaged, it is not affected by the engagements of others. A mind at peace is more powerful than a mind at war. This mind can face conflicts with the certainty that peace can disarm any reaction.

119.

To say no to that which is false is the most noble, even though the status quo may support the false. Courage is facing the overwhelming discrepancy. Most may believe the false is true and the true is false. This may require the one who stands for the truth to stand alone. Why not? Would I rather be true to myself in the midst of a multitude of deceptions or go along with this multitude because it is easier to be part of the crowd? The one who stands alone has a better chance of freeing himself from the false.

120.

The real birth is into the present which is free of time and free of fear. In the present, the holy instant is extending its peace and love. A birthday, in which we come into a new life, there is only cause for celebration and joy. Why do we slip back into the demands and constraints of time that rob us of this joy? The real birth is the death of problems and fear of problems. Within us is the capacity to be in the present without fear. In this fearless state there is love. So there is only one decision to make: to be in the present or not; to be with love or fear.

121.

The real work to do is an internal cleansing. Memories are in need of transmutation. Any anger still in the mind will prevent it from rising to freedom. The soul, composed of these energetic memories yearns to be happy and free. To be free of anger one must first take 100% responsibility for everything one experiences. No more blame or victimhood. To clear oneself totally from anger and judgment, different priorities of life are needed. To value peace above all else, contact with the Spirit is most important. This contact begins to silence one's thought. Inner peace dawns in a mind that is silent and still.

122.

In Bali the ancient Hindu culture pre-exists the tourist industry. Though it is hard to escape the lower vibrations of commercialism of the tourist industry, one cannot help to rise above it by the prevalence of Divine Worship. In the blood of the Balinese is the reverence for Nature, God, and Man. They are a joyful people, and they express this holy joy in their art, dance, sculpture, drama and batik fabrics. Temples are everywhere, and each house has some sort of small temple or altar to which the whole family pays homage. Tourism is everywhere, but so is Divine Worship.

123.

The mixture of Western technology with Eastern spirituality has produced a hybrid that is often chaotic and disharmonious. Forgiveness is needed to rise above the clash of cultures. The serenity of the indigenous culture is masked over with commercialism. The stores selling many Western items as well as Balinese handicrafts dominate the main road. There is a busy-ness that sets one on edge. The narrow streets, mixed with incessant traffic of cars and scooters are not welcoming in a beautiful way. It feels like an onslaught of activity when one leaves the hotel for the streets.

124.

At the Bonsai Villas where we are staying the suite is tranquil. There are gardens which lead up to our rooms, a pool, and wonderful bonsai trees that are very old and well developed. This art of bonsai, the art of growing miniature trees, requires careful attention. The owners of this place know how to maintain them, as they are very healthy dwarf trees. It is quite an enhancement of the small space in which the villas are placed. The scale of the trees makes the space seem much larger. This art of gardening in our villa takes away some of the chaos of the streets, thankfully.

125.

A new country is a place where opinions can be put aside and an open mind can be nourished. The people in cities who rely on the tourists for economic viability have entered a new culture. To keep up with the modernization, more money is needed. The innocence that Bali possessed 30 years ago has been displaced by commercialism. The onslaught of Western influence has transformed Bali and not always for the better. It is not simply a holy destination now, but rather a getaway for adventuresome Westerners to escape from their routine back home. Bali is on the verge of an identity crisis.

126.

Ganesh is worshipped here in Bali because the religion is primarily Hindu. The remove of obstacles is sculpted in the local stone and his presence is seen in many of the temples, large and small. Also, in the doorways to many buildings are two flanking demons. Perhaps they are to "protect" the inside with a scary nature, and keep evil from entering the abode. These guardians are often wrapped with a black and white checkered cloth, and given incense and offerings daily. The worship of these deities appears behind the scenes, but out of the corner of one's eye, an aware visitor can see locals honoring the Divine.

127.

The ornamentation on the traditional Balinese temples is dense and intricate; an interweaving of floral and geometric forms so dense there is no room for empty space. But what is very interesting is the openings to the temples. The inside surfaces of the entries are perfectly flat, as if to give the columnar space between the two sides the strong impression of a pillar of pure space. A pillar of light is akin to Lord Shiva, with no beginning or no end. But these pillars of pure space in the entries to the temples are metaphors for the vertical nature of Shiva's POWER.

128.

To be led by Divine Forces one must give up his agenda. The best directions come unexpectedly, when one is not even trying to "make things happen." Then life unfolds in its own way with a power that is beautiful and clean. All that occurs is in the Divine Plan. Providence is merely acceptance of what is. Trusting that all needs are met releases the mind from unnecessary planning. The inspiration that comes from above can only come in a state of emptiness and certainty. Faith is merely operating in the vast unknown with a trust that all will be well. In this faith is inspiration given, not sought. Every breath is then a source of gratitude.

129.

I receive what I give. Ganesh, please remove from all that I give anything but Love. If the form of my Love looks tough and confronting, please remove that tinge of attack from my voice and help me to deliver Your vision in only ways that help and soothe. Let me not assume I have a right to confront people. Let me not hurt nor cause pain. Allow me to always correct myself first, and then I may be a clear channel for your Divine Love. Please remove the obstacles to Love before I know they are there. Be my guide and my friend, a Reality to me and not just a projection of belief. Come into me and give me clear vision of my holy direction.

130.

Let me accept the truth of my innocence, bestowed to me from my Creator eons ago. I had forgotten it, but now You bring it to my awareness in full blazing light of truth. I am as You created me, so therefore I need not worry where You lead me now. I will be like a little child who trusts his father and mother to totally take care of him. You are my one Source, and I rest in you. Bring me only the vision that reinforces pure Love in me. Let me banish all fear from my mind, and live in certainty that only joy is real; all else a bad dream of my own making. Help me to correct myself. Bring me peace and joy only in this happy vision of your absolute love.

131.

The mood and feelings that I choose affect how I see the world. Today I can accept a joyous world and feel the love of God within me. Everything I receive I ask for because my thoughts are the determiners of what comes to me. Oh Ganesh, remove the thoughts I do not know I have which draw to me negative and painful experiences. Allow me to see these as opportunities to forgive. Remove from my mind all thoughts that hurt. Be my protector and friend. Bring only joy to me because You are the embodiment of joy. To You, Ganesh, I bow. Jai Ganesh!

132.

Oh Divine Mother, I am your servant for life after life, yet now do I join my wanting nature with the surrender at the feet of Your Will. Make me ever Your hands, feet, ears, and eyes. Let the fragrance of Your blessings always waft my way and the taste of Your delectable Grace be at the feast of my love for You forever. Give me the direction for my action so I am aligned perfectly with You. Remove all superfluous motion from me, and let the stillness of Your vast reality rush into me. Let the notion of death leave me completely.

133.

I am on the way home to You. Shortly will I arrive certainly at the door of Your open arms. There are all of your graces ready to embrace me in all the elements of your worldly garland of joy. You are but a small distance away now. How can I hasten my steps to the one last leap of faith over the threshold of Your immortal life? At the doorway to this gift that only You can grant, help me, Oh Mother, to enter the house that is my home, the timeless answer to all of my prayers.

134.

It is time to overcome; the instant of my journeys end upon me, and one last step to be taken by You, the guardian of my immortality. Why succumb to the prevailing winds of fate, nor all the notions of that mortal death unquestioned? It is time to overcome the strange belief that we are programmed to die. I bow to You, O Mother of the universe, Who is the manifestation of all things. You are the womb from which all life springs forth. You are the spark in me.

135.

In this vast atmosphere of thin air we fly across oceans and continents only to come home to You and all of your tender mercies of benevolence. In thin air You surround our plane and guard us as we plummet through space toward our destination so dear, to the dwelling of Your eternal Love for us. Soon these times in foreign lands will cease, and the familiar altar we have made for You will receive our adorations. Only a short distance away. Now we look toward the relief of Your comfort and peace of relaxation.

136.

People are everywhere waiting for the plane to depart, in anxious waiting for the right timing, knowing well the strong possibility of delay. And we amidst the crowd of passengers who find their patience stretched, sitting on edge surrendered to a timetable of new surprises. We may very well miss our next flight. So I pray to Ganesh to keep our motion home in flow, and allow my mind to accept the way things are. -—On the flight now, miles above the middle states of endless arid space. I accept what is, and my heart is restored to calm.

137.

Into the arms of Your delay, now considering my life's action from this moment on. To what Great Force will I give my energies, to this space of receptivity, to this calling of my highest purpose, to all Thy Good which created the Universe? I am bright in my core—and there the spark of You resides like a solar cell of radiating regency, a glorious glow of my highest aspiration. In this pause of poignant reflection, let me see my path before me, the trail that takes me well into my contribution, my inspiring words I write for You, the Master Poet of Universes.

138.

Praises to the Divine Mother of Life Everlasting. I am your voice of gratitude for this immense universe that goes forth in all directions, even beyond the stars—light years away. In those outer regions of the Great Void, I find myself bowing body-less at Your feet, to receive Your directions for my life. Where would you send me Mother? I am the one who finds Your woods soothing and Your mountains moving me towards greater heights of my being. Inspire me to be the tool of Your love on earth. Take me in Your hands and mold me into Your creation.

139.

A love for life would produce a love for Humanity, a love of Nature, and a love for the Forces that created the universe. It would not judge nor hold any grievances toward anyone or anything. All there is would be beautiful, and gratitude pervades the mind. Love of Life is the highest realization. Silence and stillness allows space to observe this very nature of existence. The essence of all things is joy. Any other association with Life is false. All the pain and suffering of my world is self-projected. Only Life is, therefore only Joy is. When Life is denied for death, all the sorrows of mankind begin.

140.

Oh Mother, I come to You with open heart and hands to serve. Grant me Your Grace of Compassion to extend to the world. Help me to reach out to those in need of Your Care. Help me to cleanse myself of all impurities within myself. Bring to me a deep inner Peace. Caress me with the dawn of soft light, and in the evening, blanket me with the shadows of a restful dusk. Bring me more into my awareness of You. Guide my actions as You see fit. I am Your servant for Life. I will sing Your Praises forever. Joy to your Son, Ganesh!

141.

The necessity in life is to remove fear from the mind. Thought by its very nature contains fear, so what is a person to do? Facing fear, which manifests as various forms of upset—anger, irritation, discontent—is the beginning of overcoming it. But the real fear to face is inside. It's not fear of wrestling with an alligator or going to war. It is fear of facing ourselves, fear of who we are. Is there guilt inside we are afraid to face? Are we afraid to accept our innocence and Holy magnitude? Usually we are. Getting to the other side of these kinds of fears is the real work.

142.

Into this little book, my Mighty Ganesh, You go by the hand of words, those touches of telepathy from the mind of Your cosmic charge—to remove all obstacles that hinder total absorption into Your Love. I beseech this Absolute Power you wield to cut through all my resistance, all my self-imposed barriers to Truth. Annihilate all my falseness. Obliterate my deceptions that fool my mind and prevent me from knowing You. I invite You totally to take over my life and lead me on Your great back to my true Self.

143.

In this journey started long ago I come close to its end. You have taken me lifetime after lifetime to the door into my Self, that last portal before the font of immortality. I am ready, my dear Remover of Obstacles, for You to take from me this last hesitation to accept myself as God created me. Bring me through this door to my Identity. End all of my delay and walk with me quickly into this light effulgent, into this Elysian field I only dreamed of before, but now presently with You is my certain destination.

144.

I see the Sun, the great giver of Light in this system of planets so small in relation to the rest of the universe. A million miles is nothing to the immensity of Creation. Man, who is even smaller, has not joined himself with this immensity, therefore has not accepted his true Source. The light of the sun is all he fathoms, and even that so sparsely. The Light of Cosmic proportions evades him. These proportions are measured by Love and Joy, not by miles and light years. He is a child of this Light. Let him now awaken! Jai Ganesh!

145.

Where there is no illusion, my God, let me go there. You send Your Great Son Ganesh, the elephant power that takes all doubt from me and pushes me forward, to lead me to the absolute Joy of my Identity in You. I sing songs of endless adoration to this power that plummets me into a new life of Divine Purpose. You lead me past all meaningless diversions that are not the real road to truth. Only You open my eyes to the Absolute. Only You grant the boon of total liberation. I bow to You, and touch the feet of my brother, Ganesh.

146.

Take from me my yesterdays. I have no more need for worn out memories of past captivity. I do not stand in the shackles of my own mistakes. I am absolved by your Love that comes to me through grace when I accept this Atonement, and extend to everyone forgiveness. We are all children of a bad dream from which I now awake. Give me that strength to forgive all in my path that Ganesh makes clear. He takes from me my weak attempts to liberate myself from doubt, and gives back to me a faith that can remove mountains of uncertainty. I ride upon Him to the sure fountain of truth.

147.

This Divine Dance You dance with me, my brother, remover of obstacles, takes those last leg holds of conflict from their stubborn grasp on the strides of my movements toward truth. So, waltz with me in the elation and delight to be one with You. Oh, Master Ganesh, my brother who has bulled through the impossible with faith of real elephant power, take over my heart and soul as You lead me to the Grace of Pure Love, Pure Joy, Pure Being in Our Divine Nature. You are the one I call in my time of need, because You erase from my mind all thoughts of need. In You am I totally fulfilled.

148.

The greatest obstacle to truth is our false belief in death. It only can pretend to be true because it puts "form" before "content," or "effect" before the real "cause." The belief in death gives great power to the body as an entity affected by forces beyond control of the mind. Yet because there is only mind that manifests form, the real cause of death is a thought. I have free will to think what I think. I can use a mind that places Life and Immortality as the cause, or I can use a mind that believes in death as an end to life. The choice is mine. I invoke Ganesh to choose Life.

149.

There is no obstacle to truth Ganesh cannot remove. For those who admit they were wrong by believing in sickness and death, or the "entropy" factor of so called scientific observations, there is the absolute power of forgiveness that restores their body, mind, and spirit into a perfect *Christed* entity. Ganesh is the One Who can take from me all false beliefs and transmute them to nothing. Nothing has no real effects. Therefore, when my belief in death is removed, the effects of a bodily death are forever removed as well.

150.

Beat the drum of truth into my heart, oh, One brother of immortality, my sibling of the Light, Who takes away all the darkened corners of my life. Touch with Your rhythmic talents those notes of negation that obliterate all obstacles to total absolution. Remove all lies that usher from lips of my falsity. Transform my heart into a vessel of Love beyond measure, one that holds all humanity in the central chamber of unlimited devotion. Bring me into Your vibrant vitality that beats in the Heart of God Itself.

151.

Ganesh, my brother, I have spent this year with You in the deepest recesses of my call to God. In the moments of despair You come rushing to greet me to change my mind to the great truth of Your Love. I am the brother to others through this example of Your determination not to leave me alone in the hell I made. Come into my heart more and more. Take over my life completely in an Action of Divine Service. Let me prove the truth of Your Love by removing the sorrow of others. Let their despair be my call now, that I may rush to remove their tears by the light of my real Self.

152.

The Ganesh Brotherhood is upon the planet now. Who can join? Anyone who wants to embrace absolute, unconditional Love as their truth. Anyone who wants to remove the obstacles of hate and judgment that separate them from knowing the truth of this Love. The Ganesh brotherhood brings all mankind together. It is beyond belief systems, church dogmas, and organizational structures and governments. It transcends all nationalities and speaks a language undivided by different dialects. It speaks only words of healing and wholeness. LOVE is its ONLY TRUTH.

153.

Into the outer regions of thought I go to that place of the mind that defies the logic of conventions and respectable appearances. This is a book for the disillusioned. Those who have investment in the systems of advantage and division will stay confined to their man-made *heavens* and *hells*. This is probably not a book for them but for those fed up with the conflicts of duality, with the belief that all life must have a "death." This little Ganesh book is for you, who read this far. I dedicate it to you who have come with me in this journey toward immortality.

154.

The completion of anything (especially a little handwritten Ganesh book, in an age of sound bites and tweets from the internet of infinite fragments of the mundane) that takes an extended attention toward matters of life and death would naturally bring Joy to the attendant. I am happy to have received the help of Ganesh, that part of my Self that comes from the determination to see something through to the end. His Joy now envelopes my life with faith to succeed. His Joy is in you, my reader, to remove all obstacles that may stand in your way. Jai Ganesh!

Other Books By Markus Ray

Miracles With My Master, Tara Singh:
Applications of A Course in Miracles

Liberation Breathing:
The Divine Mother's Gift

Odes to the Divine Mother

Spiritual Intimacy:
What You Really Want with A Mate

Babaji: My Miraculous Meetings with a Maha Avatar

Physical Immortality: How to Overcome Death

About the Author

Markus Ray received his training in the arts, holding an MFA in painting from Tyler School of Art, Temple University in Philadelphia (1980-82); his undergraduate degree is from the Cleveland Institute of Art (1973-77). Markus is also a writer and a poet who brings spirituality and sensuality together in these harmonious mediums of expression. He is the author of a major work, ***Odes To The Divine Mother***, which contains 365 prose poems in praise of the Divine Feminine Energy. Along with the Odes are his paintings and images of the Divine Mother created around the world amidst his teaching and writing mission with Sondra Ray.

Markus studied *A Course in Miracles* for 17 years (1989-2006) with pre-eminent teacher, Tara Singh, and wrote about this experience in ***Miracles With My Master, Tara Singh***. This book describes his holy relationship with Mr. Singh, and essential applications of *A Course in Miracles*.

Sondra Ray was one of the first to lecture on *ACIM* since its publication in 1976, a work which is very important to achieving Physical Immortality. Now in 2018, Markus and Sondra share together on *ACIM* here online: *bit.ly/Miracles4You*

Currently Markus writes, paints, and teaches along-side his twin flame, Sondra Ray, and maintains his artistic work on ***"Art Look" —an art lover's companion—*** at *www.markusray.com* His iconic paintings of the Masters can be seen and purchased here as well, which he often creates in front of the people in the seminars, while Sondra is lecturing on Loving Relationships, Liberation Breathing / Rebirthing, Miracle Consciousness and Physical Immortality.

Art Look: —an art lover's companion —

Ganesh in Ireland

Acknowledgement

My heartfelt thanks goes to Barbara Milbourn, an extraordinary editor as well as friend, who lovingly typed this handwritten manuscript that I scribed in a tiny little *Ganesh Journal* over the course of about a year. She helped to lift me up into the most high road of being a writer, removing any obstacles of doubt I may have had about myself, that would have placed limits on my creative writing potentials and outputs. Serving as an embodiment of Ganesh during our time in Nashville, Barbara inspired me then, as she continues to do now, in her simple and acute dedication to the written word. Truly with Barbara, in her inherently peaceful nature, the pen is more mighty than the sword. Jai Ganesh!

Notes

Printed in Great Britain
by Amazon